Shattered Glass with Glitter

Nadia King

Shattered Glass with Glitter © 2023 Nadia King

All rights reserved.

Nadia King asserts the moral right to be identified as author of this work.

Presentation by *BookLeaf Publishing*

Web: www.bookleafpub.com

E-mail: info@bookleafpub.com

ISBN: 9789357745093

First edition 2023

ACKNOWLEDGEMENT

To the one that keeps me going, even in my darkest moments. I love you 3000 Boogs.

1

Burning eruptions,
　release from me-
　pent up, boiling,
　an uncertain stance of wind
　begging-
　"Please do not blow me over,
　for I do not know if I will rise again."

　Touch of calm and destruction
　branded on glistening mounds
　I can't stop...

2

Trust

A funny little thing,
yet all sense of the word is lost.
That one last strand...
Taken, dangled in front of me, smashed
into the ground
into shattered pieces
into nothingness.

3

Sleep

Eyelids flutter like mating hummingbirds,
surrounding voices grow distant.
My body is still
as if my bones were ripped out from my body,
leaving no structure,
no support.
Repeated thoughts cause a plague.
The tickling of a warning, begging me to
submit.
The resistance is strong,
the want to succumb to eternity,
Begging for lasting relief.

Finally...

4

Lost on the road,
  no lights, no return
  devastation is certain
  help is long gone
  alone...

Darkness

5

Tendons strain
  breakage
  crumbling down and down,
  no reprieve.
  Together, broken.
  Together, broken again.
  A beat with no movement.

  A gasp of nothing!
  Silence...

6

Look at me.
  Do you see the holes?
  It was easy, wasn't it?
  the kisses,
  the touches,
  the words.

Not enough,
  no meaning?
  my kisses,
  my touches,
  my words.

The ping of the pong
  ringing constantly,
  piercing

Hate,
  loath,
  melt,
  love,
  blank

7

Stranger in the dark,
  is that you?

Why are you here?
  Don't I mean anything?
  Nothing?

Gravitational pull,
  interlocking.

I can't force myself away.

Hope

As a child,
you are told
to hold on to it with all of your might.

As an adult,
you appear
foolish as you are,
demanded to think
realistically.

Either way,

You
Lose.

9

Familiar, unknown

Passion, truth or fabrication?

Love, lies, truth

Peace, pieces

Risk, defeat

I am all in.

10

A mirror with cracked reflections,
  distorting the point of view
  visible to all
  mimicking expectations
  and smiles.

  They don't know the plastic
  behind the statue,
  the illusion in front
  of the stage.

"Come on pretty girl, the show must go on."

11

You are a Force.

I see Light.
there is calmness,
safety,
knowledge,
strength,
compassion.

Yet...

I see Dark.
there is fear,
hate,
anger,
suffering,
passion.

Choose a path...

12

I get lost
  in your eyes.

I drown
  in your words.

I wish
  upon your stars.

I crave
  your kisses and touch,

yet...

I know it isn't real.

I refuse to use a map.
I won't come up for air.
I waste all of my desires.
I feed my temptation.

I know I should stop, yet...

I will continue to sink into your abyss.

13

The beat of my heart
  produces an unfamiliar rhythm.

The breath from my lungs
  is labored,
  unsteady.

Sweat surrounds my insides,
  trying to escape,
  it remains trapped.

Butterflies migrate from
  my stomach
  on an uneasy path
  to my head.

Tense movements shake,
  uncontrollable, yet
  necessary.

Forever take a moment.

Is it over?
Does it exist?
Is it real?

14

I wish I had's
and
I'm glad I did's

You are stuck in
 the wishes,
 the maybe's,
 the possibility.

I seek pleasure in
 the moments,
 the memories,
 the magic.

I can't bring you to my side
 though I have saved a seat.

Control is relinquished
 for you,
 for me,
 for us.

The Watcher refuses to answer what if.

There is no what if.

There is nothing,
 but
 what remains.

I will keep my
 "glad I did's"
 they will comfort me
 as I push the
 wishes away.

15

I can't have you.

I try and I reason but the answer is still the
same.

I can't have you
  because you aren't mine to have.

My feelings are just breezes in the air that you
will never catch.

My heart is there,
  ready,
  but you have planned for something else.
  That date is already booked.

My words are lost on pages that you will never
read because
  the book is waiting to be published.

My smiles are for all and none, casually thrown
overboard to willing victims
  all except

You...

16

Everything has changed.

Those butterflies have turned
into memories.
Grey is sprinkled in.

Experiences have matured
but the laughter
still remains

Wrinkle tells stories
of good times and bad.

It has changed, but is everything the same?

17

My brain is shaking

Or is it my body?
My eyes?
My heart?
My ankles?

No, it can't be.

Everything is fine, everyone is fine.

But me?

No.

What is fine?
Normal?
Extreme?
Calm?

As everything spins,
darkness,
extreme light
rainbow,
grey.

Do I breathe? Do I stop?

Pins.
Needles.
Thread.

Unraveled.

Disintegrated.

I am fine....

18

She is a force
  for good,
  for truth
  for what is
  real.

Her shadow hides
  truth,
  love,
  pain,
  and hope.

The grooves on her fingers
  are a map of
  the hands she has held,
  the tears she wiped away,
  the love she has handed out.

What is left to give?

It doesn't matter, she'll try again.

19

Focus...

Clear and cool.

Driving force,
 fast
 and hard.

Build up,
 release.
 Again,
 release.

Empty...
 full...

Push
 and pull.
 More!

Twist
 and turn,
 bend
 and break.

A wave
Crash!

20

You...

Eyes,
  an undiscovered sea,
  a map of navigation.

Mind,
  rowers racing towards the finish,
  knowing what is to come,
  everything and anything.

Touch,
  a weighted blanket, secure,
  calm
  through a storm.

Passion,
  deeper than ocean ridges,
  undiscovered.

As I crash,
  I leave everything and
  take nothing.

21

A broken mirror
  can be glued
  back together
  but,
  it will never be
  as it once was.
  New prisms are
  created,
  points of view are
  altered,
  the reflection
  stays the same.

A shattered mirror
  can never
  be repaired.
  What once existed
  is gone
  yet,
  when you let
  the light in,
  the sparkle
  will allow beauty
  to shine
  through.